AF255059

It Was A Beautiful Day

and

Other Personal Quiet Miracle Stories

Raouf Mama

CONTENTS

Preface

It Was A Beautiful Day and Other Personal Quiet Miracle Stories is a collection of powerful, inspirational stories. It captures personal, life-changing moments of redemption from utter despair to radiant hope, of astonishing transmuting of sorrow into joy, agony into a song of thanksgiving. It is a celebration of our sense of the "mysterious," which Einstein called "the fundamental emotion of true art and true science." In an increasingly skeptical world, amid the rush and roar of technology, these stories echo John O' Donahue's call to all of us to "celebrate the quiet miracles that seek no attention." They are a joyous song in praise of the human capacity to marvel and to wonder.

Introduction

"People will forget what you say or what you do, but people will never forget how you made them feel" – Maya Angelou

I have had the privilege as dean of arts and sciences at Eastern Connecticut State University of working with and knowing Raouf Mama for over twenty years. It goes without saying that Raouf Mama is larger than life—a unique presence on campus, in the community, and among international story tellers.

As a scientist, I wondered why Dr. Mama asked me to write an introduction for It was a beautiful day and Other Personal Quiet Miracle Stories. But of course, it is what he would do, with his penchant for the unexpected and surprise.

The five personal stories in his latest collection abound in drama and magical experiences taking place in the rural east region of Connecticut, often called the state's "quiet corner." It is in this setting, that he spins his tales of tragedy, joy, and the unexpected kindness of strangers. Yet, the storyteller is African-born and the stories reflect his Beninese upbringing, juxtaposed with his Roman Catholic faith. These stories are simply written but give a glimpse of the fragility of life and how one act of kindness can affect so many. As a storyteller to children and as a writer, Raouf Mama takes on America at full throttle to teach and bring joy and to do his part in imparting the human experience to his new adopted country.

Raouf Mama is known for his use of poetry, music, song and dance in African storytelling to enlighten us about the wonders of nature and God around us. His African perspective is clearly present in this book of stories of everyday American life events and people. Here he emphasizes the significance of paying attention to each moment of life and what we can learn from that moment if we just pay attention to the signs of the spirit. As a result, one comes out feeling stronger and more confident that there are solutions to any problem, if one just remembers these moments of inspiration and mental clarity that life brings us. Reveling in the spiritual strength of his stories is what motivates us to tackle our problems. Just remember Raouf's struggles and how when you least expect it one can get divine and spiritual guidance to make life manageable and infinitely worthwhile.

Mama's stories urge us to acknowledge our current blessings and inspire us to continue exploring life for unexpected moments of comfort and wisdom. They help us to encounter our true self while experiencing everyday life events imbued with mystical meaning. I urge the reader to focus on what is the allegorical riddle to be solved by reading each story. How does the title focus the reader? How does the story show us how to learn from our mistakes or experiences? How is the principal character in each story transformed? And what made it possible for them to become stronger and better persons? The illustrations associated with each story, so beautifully crafted by Afarin Rahmanifar, are designed to help the reader in a journey of self-discovery, with strategic use of color and abstract realism to bring forth positive energy, inner peace and deeper understanding of life's meaning.

Throughout the book, we are led to notice bursts of mental clarity that can impact us positively throughout the rest of our lives and to thrive on those nuggets of wisdom and spiritual guidance from our connections to a higher power. We start with "The gift of our Lady" which highlights how optimism is best for navigating life, how everyday miracles can happen, and how strangers can be great resources if one has a positive outlook. What is the "gift"? Not always an object that is actually received. The take home message is not to focus only on what you are now lacking but instead to make the best of what you have to work with; and always "ask and you shall receive". Lastly, acknowledge your blessings to help you keep hope for the future; feel your honest, passionate responses to each moment of life; acknowledge that family is what matters and revel in your emerging weaknesses as teaching moments.

In "A Memorable Encounter", what makes an encounter "memorable"? Is it the power of an optimistic outlook? Is being somewhat unrealistic better in the long run? We learn that teachers touch and empower others for a lifetime. We are shown the importance of remembering how short encounters can impact one's ability to solve future life problems if one remembers those moments of clarity and acknowledges them. In "The Kindness of Strangers", one does not encounter Blanche Dubois' view of the world of always relying on the kindness of strangers to survive – but instead one is guided to revel in the kindness of strangers as the way to make one's life have greater meaning and enhance one's soul fulfillment.

In the best of the folkloric tradition, all of his stories are rich in nuances, noticing all aspects of the world around us, infusing meaning to those seconds of recognition of greatness and grace, such as "on my daughter's lips, daddy was a word of infinite beauty touched with magic". Strangers can be messengers of hope where there is despair and can bring much needed kindness to the world. As in "It Was a Beautiful Day", a recurring dream image is a beautiful lady bringing hope, solace, joy and erasing despair. As in "It is a Miracle!", he urges us to appreciate the myriad of small miracles that happen to us throughout our lives to bring comfort to any current despair, and to reflect on the wonders of love and family and your neighbors as a guide to a life well lived. Ultimately, in all his stories he exhorts us to forge our own "road to Emmaeus" form of enlightenment and to let his stories bring "good news to them that sorrow, and to them that wait in fear and anguish, hope and peace passing all understanding

A Gift Of Our Lady

I sat glum and impassive like a man devastated by a hang-over as the Paris-bound Aer Lingus flight prepared for take-off. I had left my reading glasses at home, and couldn't bear the thought of having to sit on a plane for six whole hours without reading.

For lack of anything to do, I fixed the TV screen in front of me absent-mindedly as safety instructions were being enacted. All around me, people were paging through magazines or reading books. Like me, they didn't have much time for the safety instructions. What seasoned air-traveller hadn't learned that knowing how to put on a life-jacket and exit in an emergency never made a blind bit of difference when the time came?

On previous flights, seeing men, women and children engrossed in reading had filled me with emulous zeal, but now I could scarcely bring myself to look at them. The very sight of them mocked my negligence, my absent-mindedness and envy rose to my throat like bile.

"Where are your thoughts that you are forever so forgetful?" I heard a voice whisper in my ear. The tone of gentle admonition sounded eerily familiar. I looked around instinctively, frowning. It was then my mother rose before my imagination, chin cupped in the palm of her hand, a sorrowful smile playing about her lips.

Since I was a child, my absent-mindedness had been her despair, a trial on her patience. "If your organ had not been attached to your body, child," she used to cry, shaking her head despairingly, "if your organ had not been attached to your body, you would have left it lying about and someone less fortunate than you would have grabbed it and run away with it."

Three months before her death, on the night I was returning to America after a month-long visit home, she scolded me for the last time. I had gone to the airport and left my passport I knew not where. Rushing back home to search for it, I prayed that I would find it and face the fire of mom's anxious questioning without giving myself away.

"Why have you come back from the airport?" mom asked in a tremulous voice as she heard me come in.

"Just a moment, mom," I said as I rushed into my room.

Joy and relief surged in my heart as I caught sight of my passport gleaming black on top of a pile of books.

I found mom sitting up in her sickbed, chin cupped in the palm of her hand, her face veiled in sorrow. I put my hands around her tenderly and felt her body shake with silent sobs.

"You have forgotten to take your passport or your ticket, haven't you?" She asked in a tone of gentle admonition.

I knew then that I would never be able to live with my conscience afterwards if I told her the lie I had concocted about my flight being delayed and my resistless desire to hold her close one more time.

"If your organ had not been attached to your body," she intoned, shaking her head in slow motion, a sad smile playing upon her lips, "if your organ had not been attached to your body, you would have left it lying about somewhere and someone would have stolen it."

The vision of mom scolding me on her sick bed from which alas she was never to rise again overwhelmed me with sorrow.

About an hour into the flight, I caught myself praying to the Virgin Mary. Then I saw an air hostess walking down the aisle away from me.

"Tell the lady about your glasses," a voice whispered to me.

I got up and hurried after the air-hostess.

"Excuse me Madam" I said, "I left my reading glasses at home and wonder if you happen to have onboard a supply of spare reading glasses for people in my predicament.

"I am sorry sir," she said. "We don't have spare reading glasses onboard, but when we get to Dublin, I will show you a shop where you can get a pair." But as I was turning away from her, she motioned me to wait and said: "Let me check and see if I have my spare glasses in my bag."

She returned shortly afterwards, holding up like a banner of victory a gold- rimmed pair of glasses, crying "I have found one, I have found one."

I tried them on and they were perfect.

For more than three hours I read without any sensation of strain on my eyes. "How wonderful!" I thought.

"These glasses are not my own, and yet my own would not have served me better. This is a miracle."

It was then the voice that had prompted me to talk to the air-hostess whispered to me again.

Again I got up and went in search of the lady.

"Pardon my importunities," I said. "Your glasses are a wonder. Three hours of reading and no strain on my eyes. They are better than my own. Would you be kind enough to let me buy them from you?"

"Buy them from me?" she repeated, throwing out her arms in helpless laughter. "Tell you what: you may have them."

I was beside myself with joy.

"You are most kind" I said. "I am a writer and I will give you a copy of one of my children's books as a token of my gratitude."

"I love to read," she exclaimed, "and I would be delighted to have one of your books.!"

I rushed back to my seat, rummaged in my briefcase for a copy of *Why Monkeys Live In Trees*.

"By the way, I am Raouf," I said. "I need to autograph the book. What's your name?"

"I am Mary," she said. Her voice had a tone of unaccustomed tenderness and the smile upon her face was a mask of dazzling light. "Mary," I said, shivering in rapture. And I felt an impulse to go down on my knees and cry out to her: "Blessed are you among women," but a voice whispered to me, "not here, not now."

By a stern effort of will, I held the impulse in check and said simply. "God bless you Mary."

"God bless you," she said, holding me in her gaze a moment.

I went back to my seat like a man walking on air.

A Memorable Encounter

I rushed out of the auditorium and jumped into my car, the voices of the children still ringing in my ears.

"Dr. Mama, Why did you take your shoes off for story-time?"

"Dr. Mama, Is your name really Mother?"

"Dr. Mama, how many languages do you speak?"

"Dr. Mama, could we do the African dance one more time? It's really cool"

The storytelling at Killingly Elementary School had gone very well that morning, so well in fact that I had forgotten all about the time constraints I was under. Now I was in trouble, for I had only an hour and a half to get to Lawrence State College, where I was going to deliver a keynote address, whereas I would need at least an hour and forty-five minutes to drive there.

"Desperate ills call for desperate remedies," I thought to myself as I started the engine and drove off like a man pursued by the very devil himself. On the highway, I revved the engine until the needle of the speedometer hovered near 80.

I shot a glance at my watch. Time was flying whereas I was just creeping along. Gritting my teeth, I stepped hard on the pedal and watched the needle go down, and down until it came to rest against the 110 miles per hour marker, waving now and then like a cobra preparing to strike.

I knew that what I was doing was wrong, wrong and illegal, but it never occurred to me that I could die if I blew a tire. The only thing I was worried about was getting caught, for I knew the police could suspend my driver's license. And that to me was the ultimate horror. How would I get from home to school if I couldn't drive? How would I get from one place to another in my daily round of errands? How would I drive to various venues for storytelling, an activity which had grown into a second job, a necessary second source of income?

But not even the fear of losing my driver's license was strong enough to bring me back to my senses.

Having got my driver's license barely two years before after three failed attempts, I was foolish enough to think I could catch any police cruiser before they would catch me provided I stayed alert. I had yet to learn that police cruisers had a habit of lurking in ambush for such foolish, reckless drivers as myself and were equipped with radars powerful enough to monitor traffic miles and miles away.

"It is not illegal to break the law," I murmured to myself, rather like Fagin egging Oliver on. "What's illegal is to get caught breaking the law."

For a few moments, I thought I was flying through the air, wrapped in a cloak of invincibility. I was hugging the fast lane to myself, overtaking in a blur a never- ending stream of cars, with some of the drivers shaking their heads or honking their horns.

"Press the pedal to the metal, boy, press the pedal to the metal," I shouted in defiance, gripping the wheel hard and keeping my gaze fixed straight ahead for any sign of a police cruiser. But my watchfulness seemed an unnecessary precaution, for as far as I could tell the police had taken the day off, the road was my oyster and my car, my sword.

It was then I saw it in my rear view mirror, an unmarked police cruiser with its lights flashing.

"I hope it's not me he's after," I said, feeling giddy with fear, my heart thumping in my ears.

I bore right towards the slow lane and to my horror saw the cruiser get right on my tail.

"Driver's license, please," the police officer said gruffly, almost snapping his fingers in impatience.

"And what's the hurry," he added, as I pulled the card out of my wallet, my hand shaking.

"I am sorry, but I have a keynote address in less than half an hour and I am running late."

The man glared at me a moment and then yanked the card out of my hand, as if to say "Keynote address indeed… Give me the damned thing."

I watched him stomp back to his cruiser, a tall, imposing figure, bigger and fiercer than any police officer I had ever seen.

"I am done for" I whimpered, my eyes misting over. This man will take my driver's license away, and I will not be allowed to drive for a long time to come. What am I to do?"

Clenching my fists, I launched into prayer, reciting the Lord's Prayer and the Hail Mary over and over and over. The tick-tock of my wrist watch sounded loud in my ears, like a time bomb ticking away to the implosion of my career as a teacher and a storyteller.

I waited five, six, seven, eight whole minutes, my eyes glued to the rear view mirror and still the man remained in his cruiser.

When at last he came out and walked towards me, I thought I saw the ghost of a smile playing about his lips.

"What can the bugger be smiling about!" I fumed in impotent rage. "This man has been so schooled in cruelty that the prospect of depriving me of my driver's license and destroying my career fills him with glee." "We shall see about that."

For a moment we fixed each other, and I was determined to look defiant and undaunted, but what I saw in his eyes was neither spite nor cruelty but sadness, and I bowed my head in shame.

"Shame on you" he said at last. "You a professor and you behave like this on the highway? If you go on like this, you will never get to your venue in one piece. If I ever catch you at it again, sir, I will have to suspend your driver's license and have you go back to driving school. Do you hear me?"

"I hear you, sir," I said meekly, moved almost to tears by the man's unexpected kindness. "I promise I will never do this again."

"That's what every reckless driver says when he or she gets caught," he replied, handing me my driver's license, a gentle smile creasing the corners of his eyes.

He stepped back and raised his hand half in salute and half in farewell.

"By the way," he said, "I was a student at Eastern Connecticut State University. The University needs you, young man; this country needs you, and your family needs you. Drive safely, please."

Before I could find the words to thank him, he was gone, but his words have stayed with me all these years. Like stars in the dome of heaven, they do not come up when my mental sky is bright with sunshine, only when the sun is out of sight and I feel the beast in the jungle egging me on to a reckless or foolish deed. It is then I remember and step back from the brink.

It Is A Miracle!

"I think there are two babies breathing here, not one," my wife said, patting her belly gingerly, her large, brown eyes fixed on me to gauge my reaction.

"You must be joking," I said, trying not to sound hysterical, my heart beating like a drum at the hands of a demented drummer.

I passed my hand over the spot she had indicated, frowning, hoping against hope that she was just trying to scare me.

Twins were considered demi-gods in the country where we came from, and Iya- Bedji, Mother of twins, and Baba-Bedji, father of twins, were appellations generally regarded as one of the crowning glories of parenthood. It was fear my wife's announcement aroused in me, however, not joy, for I knew not how on earth we were going to cope with the addition of twins to the three girls we had been struggling to raise as a young couple in America.

"You'd better believe it," Aissa said with a deep sigh, her shoulders sagging as though giving way under a heavy load, a painful smile hovering over her lips. Then, burying her face in her hands, she broke down and wept like a child.

This woman, to whom my innermost thoughts were an open book, this woman whom I had promised on our wedding night to protect, to cherish and to hold forever and ever was more worried, more scared than I was; and I desperately wanted to take the fear and the worries away from her and bury them deep within myself.

"Don't cry," I said, throwing my arms around her, gently leaning my head against hers in the manner of traditional healers gifted with the power to relieve headache by osmosis. "Where you and I come from, the birth of twins is a blessing from God. Before long, you will be called Iya-Bedji—mother of twins, and I Baba-Bedji —father of twins. Joy and hope should fill our hearts as we prepare for the coming of these children, not fear and worry."

"I know," she said, struggling to swallow her sobs. "I know I shouldn't feel the way I feel. I know that the coming of twins is cause for rejoicing, and yet, and yet…"And her voice was choked with tears.

Days turned into weeks and weeks into months and our initial fears and worries gave way to joyful expectations. In the course of the fifth or sixth month, the doctor told us that the twins were boys. My wife and I were beside ourselves with joy. We wanted a boy after begetting three girls one after another and God was giving us two! He was indeed Beneficent!

But then Aissa came back from a doctor's appointment one day about twelve weeks before her due date in tears. The doctor had informed her that she would soon have to be put on complete bed rest to protect her and forestall the risk of premature births!

"The doctor said I would have to be confined to bed until my due date for my own safety and to save the babies from being born before their time," she said, her voice breaking with desperation.

"Who will take care of our three girls? Who will take care of me? And what about the thousand and one chores which need to be done around the house? You will have to quit your job and stay home all day every day until the babies are born."

I stared at her in bewilderment, numb with fear and worry, nodding again and again, unable to utter a single word of comfort.

And there came upon me a sudden impulse to run away, far, far away and hide in a remote corner of the earth beyond the reach of family worries and responsibilities.

She clutched my hands fiercely and looked beseechingly into my eyes, her face bathed in tears. "You won't run away and leave me and the children in the lurch, will you?"

"Whatever has put such a silly idea in your head!" I cried in horror, terrified at the accuracy of her words. "Only a monster would do such a thing!"

"I am sorry," she said with tears in her voice, "I am very sorry. I am losing my head."

Never has an apology filled with greater shame the one it was meant to soothe.

"Everything will be all right," I said, pressing her gently to me and averting my eyes so she wouldn't see my shame. My voice seemed not my own but that of a ventriloquist hiding behind me. "Believe you me, all will be well."

Within three weeks, my wife and I managed, we knew not how, to pay for her mother to come over from our home country and help us out in our hour of need. An angel of mercy could not have outdone that woman in her devotion to our family. Nurse, housekeeper, cook, babysitter, mother and grandmother all rolled up into one, she worked tirelessly from dawn far into the night. In no time at all my worries and my fears seemed no more than bad dreams dimly remembered, my household was once again on an even keel, and I felt as though it was going to be plain-sailing all the way to the births of the twin boys.

But then, Aissa went to the doctor for a check-up a little over a week before her due date. I was about to call her from my office to ask what the doctor had said when the phone rang.

"You have beaten me to the phone by a split second," I cried. "I was just about to call you when the phone rang."

"Yah… Yah…" she said a little impatiently before proceeding to tell me what the doctor had said. I heard her out, but as it turned out, what she had said was one thing and what I had heard was quite another.

"So the doctor said everything is all right and the twin boys will be delivered on schedule," I said by way of confirming what I had heard her say.

But instead a "Oun-houn" of agreement, Aissa went off like a bombshell.

"What did l just tell you?" She screamed. "That the doctor said that the boys are breached and will have to be delivered by caesarian section, but you weren't listening, were you? That has been the story of my life as a married woman. You simply never listen to me. Whatever I say to you is wasted breath. It goes in one ear and out the other."

She paused for breath and I filled the interval with desperate apologies. But it seemed as though she had had it with me. "Have a good day" she said icily and hung up on me.

A few days before her due date, the doctor summoned Aissa back to his office. This time, I made a point of being present.

"I wanted to check the position of the kids one more time before I schedule the Caesarian operation, just in case," the doctor said in a tired voice that felt like icy fingers tracing my spine, "but the likelihood of any change in their position is slight. Still, one never knows."

I paced the waiting room back and forth, biting my lips as the doctor did the check-up, my imagination swarming with all kinds of doom-laden complications of the operation I was convinced was now on the cards.

I did not bother to pray. All I wanted to do was beat my fists against the wall and curse my fate. Only by a superhuman effort of will did I keep the impulse in check.

Suddenly the door to the examination room opened wide and the doctor rushed out smiling broadly. "It's a miracle," he cried, his eyes gleaming bright. I couldn't believe it, but there it was, clear as daylight. The twin boys have shifted their positions at the eleventh hour and eliminated the need for a Caesarian section. Congratulations!"

I clasped the doctor's hand in a warm, prolonged handshake and then threw my arms around my wife, hugging her close and showering her with kisses and congratulations. I knew I was wide awake. I knew the doctor's kind words and joyful handshake, my beautiful Aissa' s sweet embrace, the bright smiles flashing all around like so many reporters' cameras swinging into action to capture the magic of the moment—I knew all these were as real as the polished floor beneath my feet and the vaulted ceiling over my head. And yet it felt like a dream.

And it came to me that what my wife and I had experienced over the past nine months was the stuff of dreams: twin male children conceived after the successive births of three girls, the ordeal of a 12 week bed rest passing off without mishap, the eleventh hour shift in the twin boys' positions from "breached" to "normal"—these belonged in the realm of miracles and were cause for thanksgiving.

It was then I decided that one of the twin boys would be named Raman and the other Rahim in praise of Him whose love passes all understanding, the Most Merciful, the Most Beneficent. And these are the names the twin boys have borne to this day.

It Was A Beautiful Day

The air was crisp and scented with the perfume of fresh-mown grass. The sun was shining bright in a clear, blue sky. It was a beautiful day, perfect for Father's day. All day long, I had sung songs of praise and thanksgiving, my heart dancing with joy as the tribute my children had paid me one Father' s Day after another ran through my mind again and again. "I love you dad. You are the best Dad in the whole wide world." What greater tribute can a child pay to his or her father than this? In the three years since their mother had demanded a divorce and forced me out of our home, I had known unutterable financial hardship. I had known the bitter sting of the lash of slander and malicious gossip. I had known the bitter sorrow of finding myself alone, all alone, at Thanksgiving and at Christmas. Though guiltless, I had been handcuffed and shackled like a common criminal and sent to jail for three days; but as I faced one ordeal after another, my children's love sustained and shielded me from the demons that drive men to take their own lives or seek refuge in drink or drugs.

"Count your blessings and call them by name one by one," says the poet. If children are indeed God's greatest blessings, as a popular Yoruba folksong suggests, then I am blessed beyond deserving: One daughter a graduate of one of Massachusetts' top universities and an award-winning school-teacher, the other two pursuing their studies at one of the nation's most prestigious Black colleges, their younger twin brothers just one year shy of graduating high school and going off to college.

All five siblings gifted with grace, beauty, glittering talents, magnetic personalities and a kind heart! So long as they are safe and happy, I would account myself the happiest man on the face of the earth.

I got into my car and drove along Route 32 in a buoyant mood, chatting merrily with my companion Gonzalo on the way to the house of my twin son' s coach in Norwich where my son was going to wait for me upon his return from a basketball tournament in Massachusetts. I had dropped him off at the same place two days earlier. Before hugging me goodbye, he had told me in a voice breaking with emotion that there was something wrong with him going to Massachusetts to play basketball on Father's Day. "Don't worry," I told him cheerily, "we will have our Father's Day dinner with your twin brother at your favorite Chinese restaurant in the evening. And it will be as much a celebration of Father's Day as a celebration of your team's victory over its rivals."

He flashed me a sad, beautiful smile, gave me a victory sign, and we parted company.

The text message he had sent me by cellphone shortly before I set out for Norwich to fetch him had left me in no doubt that the dinner we had planned for later that evening was indeed going to be a dual celebration. "Hit the road now, Dad. We're only 20 minutes away from coach's house. Tournament went very well. Scored a lot of points. Dunked a few times. See u soon. Love u.

I glanced at the clock. It was 7:15 PM. "The celebration dinner will have to be postponed until Thursday or Friday, for there is no way we we're going to make it to the restaurant in Manchester before it closes at 9:30 PM," I said with a sigh.

"What a chame!" Gonzalo exclaimed with a comical Hispanic accent, gesturing wildly and pulling a face of mock disappointment. "I am bery hongry."

"You are funny," I said, and we both exploded into laughter.

It was then we came upon the scene of an accident at a bend in the road, barely five minutes away from our destination. Two cars, one a truck, the other a small front-wheel-drive Nissan, had crashed into one another and veered apart. The road, strewn with broken glass and twisted pieces of plastic and metal, was impassable. A small crowd of people was milling about. Neither the police nor the ambulance was anywhere to be seen.

All of a sudden, I felt numb all over. "Something bad happened here," I said, my heart racing.

"Madre de Dios," Gonzalo moaned, his eyes widening in terror.

In my rear view mirror, I saw cars turning round and driving away.

"Let's go see what's going on and call 911 if no one has called already," I said, motioning to Gonzalo to get out.

It was then I saw, in my mind's eye, Rahim running, running towards me, in a phantasmagorical display of speed without motion.

"Rahim is in this accident" I screamed and went rushing forward. I saw two of his teammates stretched out on the ground with various injuries. A drunk driver had come hurtling round the bend, lost control, and smashed his car into the driver's side of the car they were in.

"Where is Rahim?" I gasped.

"Still in the car," one of them said. The words went through me like a knife.

"Oh, my son," I howled, and went flying over to the car. In the back-seat on the driver's side I found Rahim, motionless, his arms askew, his head resting precariously against the seat. His lower lip was puffed up, both his eyes were closed, the left one was swollen.

"Rahim," I cried, catching hold of his hand and squeezing it gently, "please answer me, answer me please!"

I felt cold, very cold.

"My son, my son is dead!" I howled, taking my head in both hands.

Gonzalo gave me a tearful, sorrowful look. "Let's get him out of the car; it may catch fire," he said.

I threw my arms around Rahim and with Gonzalo's help, pulled him out ever so gently and laid him on the grass a safe distance away.

Gonzalo laid his hand gently upon my shoulder, I as stood over my son's body, weeping without tears, shivering and moaning incoherently.

Under the spell of grief, I cried out, raising both hands to heaven imploringly "Let this bitter cup pass from me, oh Lord. Let the child live and take me instead, but your Will be done, not mine, Lord."

It was then a man drew near to me, and said in a voice full of tears: "I hope your son lives, I hope this is not the end. Three years ago my daughter was drugged and raped to death."

His words sent shivers down my back, and out of the depths of my sorrow, I reached out and took his hands in my hands. "May God comfort you in your sorrow," I said, "and may He rest your daughter's soul."

My son was rushed shortly thereafter to Backus Hospital. I drove over there I knew not how, and waiting for the doctor to come out of the emergency room to tell me about my son was agony beyond human endurance.

If my worst fear should come true, how was I going to break the heart-breaking news to Rahim's mother, to his twin-brother, or to his three sisters? In my country, the news of the death of a son, a daughter, a sibling or a close relative was never broken point-blank. Such a task could only be discharged by community elders and leaders who had mastered the art of gentle and tactful eloquence in the breaking of doleful news, but this was America, not Africa, and I would have to shoulder the grim task alone and unaided. How on earth was I going to do it?

Six years earlier, I had read out a sorrowful poem by W. H. Auden during a memorial service for my editor and publisher, Mr. Sandy Taylor, a great poet and man of letters who had taken me under his wing out of the kindness of his heart. Lines of the poem came back to me like an old friend come to keep me company in my hour of need:

Let aeroplanes circle moaning overhead
Scribbling on the sky the message He Is Dead,…
The stars are not wanted now: put out every one;
Pack up the moon and dismantle the sun.….
For nothing now can ever come to any good.

"You should call Rahim's brother or somebody," Gonzalo said. "They must be wondering what keeps him, why he hasn't got back home by now."

"Call Rahim's brother or somebody," I repeated nodding. "Yes, that's what I must do."

So I called Raman on his cell phone and told him about the accident. "What!" he cried out, "I will hand the phone over to mum."

"No," I said, "just tell her what I told you. I will call again after the doctor attending him comes out of the emergency room."

But he handed the phone over to his mother anyway, and speaking as calmly as I could, I told her briefly about the accident and told her I would call again as soon as I spoke to the doctor in the emergency room.

She was still screaming when I rang off.

When at last the doctor came to me, he held out a glimmer of hope.

"Your son is alive, not dead, but he has sustained a very serious brain injury," he said. "His brain is spotted with blood all over, similar to a shaken baby syndrome. Recovery, when it comes, will be a very long process. The next 48 hours will be critical. Any swelling of the brain will be a game-changer. Here at Backus Hospital we have neither the equipment nor the expertise to take care of him. He will therefore have to be airlifted to one of four hospitals for treatment: Yale, Hartford, Providence or Worcester."

Quickly, I went over the list in my mind. Hartford was the closest. "Hartford…

Send him to Hartford Hospital please," said I "and would you please call his mother and calm her down?.... Here is the number to call."

Gonzalo and I rushed back home, changed our shirts, and set out for Hartford.

In a dimly lit room in the intensive care unit I found my son in a coma, a mask covering his face, tubes sticking out of everywhere. I fell to my knees, caught hold of his hand and burst into tears.

Life had shown me its claws and came near to making me curse God lately, but never until now had I had to contemplate the death of my offspring.

I had borne a great many ordeals and moved on. But the death of my son! Oh God, how does one bear it and move on?

From outside the room, Gonzalo called out to me. "Ralph, do not cry, he will be ok, God willing." I turned my head and through my tears I saw his tears. "God willing," I repeated after him, the tears flowing ever more freely down my cheeks and soaking my shirt. "He will be ok, God willing."

I went to bed as dawn was breaking. And as I lay sleeping, I was transported by the hallucinatory power of dreams to a corner of my son's hospital room and found myself gazing in unutterable joy at a lady of regal presence tending to my son and giving him an injection in the left foot. She was dressed in sparkling white. Her figure, radiant as the moon, flooded the room with soft, soothing light. Her face was turned away from me, but I felt no need to look, only joy and peace passing all understanding.

I woke up at 8 to the sound of the alarm clock and instinctively went down on my knees in prayer and thanksgiving, for I knew, though I was still very afraid, I knew that my dream was a game-changer; I knew that all would be well.

I had only slept for three and a half hours and felt like going back to bed, but I had a storytelling engagement at 9 AM. Should I call the school and tell them I was sorry but wasn't up to telling stories after what had happened to my son? But the students had been looking forward to my visit these past three months, and calling the program off with less than an hour's advance notice would be the wrong thing to do.

So I took a quick shower and headed for the school. The children were delighted to see me and broke into cheers as I stepped up to the podium. For an hour or so I told stories to a jubilant audience of students and staff, gave them riddles to solve, sang to them and danced with them. It was only at our parting that I told them about my son's accident and asked them to keep him and our family in their prayers. The outpouring of love and compassion my words triggered brought tears to my eyes.

On my way to the hospital, the dream I had had at dawn came back to me and all of a sudden I felt hope, a great sense of promise rising, rising in me like a new dawn breaking. And just as sunlight puts the shades of night to flight, the fear and the sorrow that had filled my heart since the night before gave way to joy and an inexpressible sense of inner peace.

I found a big crowd of friends and well-wishers gathered in the visitors' lounge awaiting their turn to be let into my son's room, most bearing flowers, all looking sad and forlorn. Never had a hospital lounge looked more like a house of mourning. As I greeted them, I was filled with a great fervor to bear witness to the vision and the dream, and like the apostles to whom Jesus had revealed himself on the road to Emmaus, bring good news to them that sorrow, and to them that wait in fear and anguish, hope and peace passing all understanding.

Speaking in a gentle voice quivering with the fervor of the muezzin's call to prayer, I told them about the dream I had had and the vision of the Lady in sparkling white.

"Fear not." I concluded with tears in my eyes. "Have faith. That boy will pull through. Just you wait and see."

Three days later, at the hour that had been appointed for my encounter with the doctor in charge of the care of my son for the day, a lady dressed in white walked into the waiting room. Tall and spare, her complexion was a blending of ivory and ebony. "I am Doctor Joseph… the lead doctor for the team taking care of Rahim," she said, as she extended her hand in greeting, a warm smile disclosing a row of pearly white teeth. The name filled me with wonder, and all of a sudden I was carried on the wings of memory back into the presence of the Lady dressed in sparkling white tending my son in his hospital bed. Only, now she held my hand in her hand, and her face was no longer hidden from me but beaming upon me a smile beautiful beyond any singing of it. "Good morning Doctor Joseph," I said, snapping out of my trance, my heart thumping against my chest, my hand gripping her hand as though to prevent her from melting into thin air. "God bless you."

"God bless you too," she said, smiling, and led the way to her office.

"Your son has made wonderful, astonishing progress," she said. "Given the kind of traumatic brain injury he had sustained, this is nothing short of a miracle. I will order him to be discharged in three or four days. He will have to check into a rehab center where he will stay until a team of experts gives him clearance to return home, which I expect will be soon. He will of course have to be monitored by a neurologist and undergo physical therapy for a while, but your son is out of danger now and well on his way to full recovery…."

Full recovery! Heavens above! A new lease on life with no mental, emotional or physical impairment whatsoever! In my ear, the phrase had a charm, a magic all its own, and I turned it over and over in my mind, like a child licking a delicious candy languorously, delicately, so he could savor it forever and ever.

I was delirious with joy, and would have fallen, weeping at her feet, but fear of embarrassing her checked the impulse. "God bless you, Dr. Joseph," I said instead. "God bless you all the days of your life."

A few days later, my son was discharged from the hospital. On our way to Gaylord Rehab Center where Dr. Joseph had decided he was going to stay for a while, my son told me something that had stayed with me ever since.

"When I was in a coma, I had the strangest, most beautiful dream ever," he said. "I was sitting by the bank of a calmly flowing river on a mild day. A dog was by my side, and both the dog and I were still and calm as we sat there, watching the river flow by. Then I was awoken by footsteps and voices."

The story gave me goose bumps and we both were quiet awhile. Then I said, "You who get bored so easily and cannot sit still for a quarter of an hour, how did you feel sitting like that, indefinitely?"

"I told you Dad," he said, with a gentle smile. "It was beautiful. I had no sense of time passing. I had no worries, no errands to run, no homework to do, no basketball games to play. And you know I love dogs.

Sitting there with my dog beside me and watching the river flow peacefully by filled me with great joy."

I nodded, again and again as there flashed upon my mind the image of me, his mother, and his siblings wailing and tearing our hair out by its roots while he

was sitting with his dog on a river bank where no mortal feet may tread, watching the river flow past.

My son and I remained deep in thought awhile. Then, as though to break the silence, he played on his MP3 a song I had never heard before, but which made such a deep impression on me I wept all the way to the rehab hospital more than 30 miles away.

> *When I am down and oh my soul so weary*
> *When troubles come and my heart burdened be*
> *Then I am still and wait here in the silence*
> *Until you come and stay a while with me*
> *You raise me up so I can stand on mountains*
> *You raise me up to walk on stormy seas*
> *I am strong when I am on your shoulders*
> *You raise me up to more than I can be.*

Within five days, two weeks to the day since his near-fatal brain injury on Father's Day, Rahim was given a clean bill of health by a team of distinguished neurologists and discharged from Gaylord Rehab

Hospital. "That boy has been touched by an angel," Gonzalo crooned, his eyes dancing like points of light on water, when I told him the news. "Touched by an angel of light, truly."

Dressed in my Sunday best, my car washed and waxed to a dazzling sheen, I set out to fetch my son. The sky was just as clear as it was two weeks earlier on Father's Day, the air just as sweet, the day brighter still; but the joy that lifted and brightened my heart on that day, poetry and oratory will labor in vain to capture. One would have to envision the ecstasy the apostles must have felt after the agony of Good Friday, to get the full measure of my felicity.

The Kindness Of Strangers

I looked on with a joyless smile as my seven year old daughter planted a sonorous kiss on each of her mother's cheeks and came skipping into my open arms, a precious dimple pitting either side of her seraphic face.

"Daddy, let's go," she piped, clutching my hand. "The school bus will soon be here! Let's hurry!"

On my daughter's lips, *daddy* was a word of infinite beauty touched with magic, and the knowledge that I was the only human being on whom that beautiful little girl had bestowed that name had always made my heart sing. There was no song in me that morning, however. I had got out of bed on the wrong side and an unnamable sadness filled my heart.

I nodded again and again, mechanically, in response to my daughter's joyful, rapid-fire prattle as we rushed down two flights of stairs and came out into the sweet early morning air.

"Quick, daddy, tell me a story or a poem before the bus comes!" my daughter crooned, clapping her hands eagerly as she scanned the deserted street.

For five minutes or so every morning since my daughter had started elementary school, I would tell her a story or recite a poem or two while she and I waited for her bus. It was a ritual both of us had come to cherish as a special parting gift. The words "quick, daddy, tell me a story or a poem before the bus comes," had been invested by both of us with the same magic as the phrase that gave Ali Baba access to the treasure-trove.

My daughter waited impatiently, fixing me with bright, dancing eyes as I searched my mind for a story or a poem. A frown soon darkened her face and she shook my hands as though to wake me from sleep.

"Daa-ddyy, come on, tell me a story or a poem. The bus will be here soon and it would be too late!" she pleaded.

Like a man in a trance, I opened my mouth and the words came rolling off my tongue:

Come away oh human child
To the waters and the wild
With a fairy hand in hand,
For the world is more full of weeping than you can understand.

"Oh daddy!" my daughter wailed, snatching up my hands and squeezing them tight, her eyes boring into mine. "That's a very sad poem. Are you all right?"

I felt the sting of tears in my eyelids and a great superstitious fear came over me, for I remembered my father had told me that it was bad luck for a little child to see his or her father cry.

"There is nothing wrong with me my dear," I lied, averting my face, struggling to force the tears back.

I regained my composure by sheer will-power, flashed her a sad, apologetic smile and, stroking her lustrous, black hair ever so gently, I went on: "That was the wrong poem to recite on a beautiful day such as this, wasn't it? I Let me see… Once upon a time, Frog and Turtle were friends…."

It was then the school bus loomed into view, and before I could retell her favorite trickster tale and make her shriek with laughter, my daughter had to go.

I saw her seated at the window, fixing me with a sad, sorrowful look, sucking on the thumb of one hand and waving to me with the other. The opening line of a long forgotten poem by Heine sprang unbidden to my lips as I waved her goodbye with both hands. It was a poem my German high school teacher had taught my class, and whose melancholy beauty made a deep impression on me at the time.

"Ich weiss nicht was soll es bedeuten dass ich so traurig bin." I know not if there is a reason why I am so sad at heart."

I loved the poem so much that the teacher made me stand up in front of the class and recite it one morning to show my classmates "how to declaim a poem with feeling," as he put it. It was all play-acting of course, for I was in the bloom of youth and sorrow was still alien to me. Much water had flowed under the bridge since then, and I had learned with tears in my eyes that *the beauty of life had two faces, one of joy, one of sorrow, cutting the heart asunder.* Of the beloved poem, however, only a fragment could I recall now though no poem could have suited my mood more perfectly as I stood waving to my little daughter, my face wreathed in a smile which had neither hope nor joy.

The bus rounded a bend and was lost to sight and I made my way to the neighborhood convenience store to buy a calling card to call my mother, whom I had missed cruelly since coming to America. Whenever I was sad or worried about what the future held, only her voice, telling me that every beat of her heart was a prayer and a blessing for me could revive my spirits and fill my heart with joy again.

I joined the long line at the check-out counter and awaited my turn. The store assistant, a tall, lanky fellow of light skin and pleasant features, seemed a little unsure of himself, judging from the fleeting frown that gathered upon his brow now and then as he listened to queries or checked IDs as a safeguard against frauds.

"This is probably his first day at the job, poor thing" I thought to myself before turning my mind to the call I was going to make and the conversation I was going to have with mom.

I knew she would surmise from the tone of my voice, however hard I might try to deceive her, that I was not happy, but what I should tell her was the cause of my sadness was something I had yet to figure out.

What on earth was I going to tell her?, "I am very sad, mom, but I do not know what it is that has made me sad?" I smiled at the incongruity of such a response, which reminded me of Polythemus saying in response to his fellow Cyclops' queries after Odysseus had driven a stake through his eye: "Nobody has hurt me!"

I had certainly had my share of sorrows in the years since I took a tearful leave of her and flew to America. The sudden death of my best friend, Fayad, run over by a drunk driver shortly before Christmas, my inability, for lack of money, to go back to my country every year to visit friends and family and take a break from the stresses and strains of life in America; my failure to get the job I had set my heart on since my college years, translating at the UN—these had been a source of great pain to me; but if I had suffered much, I also had much to be thankful for:

A Ph.D. from one of the top universities in the US, a tenure track position as a professor of English, my fourth language, a beautiful daughter, smart and articulate beyond her years, whom I loved above all else and who loved me in equal measure, excellent health and a future that spread out before me like a land of dreams—these surely are blessings that could make me the envy of multitudes!

There was more joy than sorrow in my life, to be sure, and mom would plead with me never to forget for an instant how blessed I was; yet I could not shake off the load of sadness pressing down on me.

I was jolted out of my musings by the voice of the store assistant crying out in joyful surprise and flashing a radiant smile at me. "Is this you in the flesh or am I seeing a vision! I have prayed for you every day for the past two years, man! Prayed on bended knee with tears of gratitude in my eyes!"

I drew back in shock and bewilderment, frowning as I scrutinized the man's kindly, benevolent face in a vain attempt to place him, hoping against hope that the joyful smile and the extraordinary, benevolent words were not the symptom of a sudden attack of euphoria or the opening scene of a comedy of mistaken identity.

"Who are you?" I stammered, my heart thumping against my chest.

"Ah, you do not recognize me," the man said with lights in his eyes, his voice soothing like a soft breeze. "Let me explain:"

Two years ago I was a wreck, wheelchair-bound and jobless. One day I was so hungry I decided I was going to turn to begging. I was in my wheelchair at the park across the street, pretending to be watching children at play. You walked by, dressed in your beautiful African clothes and I felt an impulse to put out my hand and beg you for money, but something held me back. You looked at me and I looked at you, then I averted my gaze and fought back my tears. You came closer, smiled at me and handed me a five-dollar bill. Man, those five dollars were more than five million dollars to me! A few months later, miraculously, I recovered from the disease that had confined me to a wheelchair, and I decided to pursue my studies and have been working on an associate degree for about a year now. I have just been offered this job. Whenever I look back on my life over the past two years, I remember the day we met, I remember your kindness to me, a perfect example of the kindness of strangers. You brought me hope that day and renewed my faith in God, and He has worked a great miracle in my life and turned it around!

So you see, your kindness has changed my life and that is why I pray for you every day. God bless you, man!

"Wow, quite a story!" a deep, gravelly voice said at my back.

"Sorry guys, I had to tell this good man how he touched my life," the store assistant said, gesturing apologetically to the multitude who had waited patiently while he spoke to me.

"No apologies needed," a frowsy, elderly woman at the end of the line replied in a voice sweet as music. "You have cast a spell on us all."

"Chicken soup for the soul," another woman cried, nodding again and again, backing her words with a thumbs-up sign.

I looked all around in a daze. Everyone was nodding and smiling at me. I nodded and smiled in return while a storm of emotions was rising in me.

I felt joy at hearing a long-forgotten stranger to whom I happened to show kindness once tell me he had prayed for me every day,

I felt sorrow at not having given him 20, 50 or even 100 dollars instead of 5, I felt a sense of wonder at the timing of our reunion and the words he spoke.

I felt gratitude at having been made a messenger of hope where there was despair.

Above all, I felt humbled by how richly the paltry alms I once gave a stranger had been repaid.

A new language would have to be fashioned to capture in words the symphony of such feelings as these.

I turned to the man again and he handed me ten calling cards, ten times as many as I had paid for, and gave me a big hug. I nodded again and again and hurried out of the store lest I lose control of my emotions and collapse in tears.

"My God! Are you all right?" Connie the secretary exclaimed, raising both hands to her mouth when I walked into the English department office and waved to her in greeting. "Were you mugged or something?"

"Mugged!" I cried, laughing uproariously, "nay, not so…blessed rather, blessed beyond all imagining! And I went into my office to count my blessings and call mom in celebration. Then I went home to await my daughter's return. "It's a beautiful story Dad!" my daughter crooned when I told her the story of my adventure with the store assistant. Upon her face there was a smile such as angels alone bring to the faces of children fast asleep.